WOW!
Look what's in
Space

KINGFISHER
LONDON & NEW YORK

The author dedicates this book to Edith Anna Lee

Copyright © Macmillan Publishers
International Ltd. 2020
Published in the United States by Kingfisher,
120 Broadway, New York, NY 10271
Kingfisher is an imprint of Macmillan Children's Books, London
All rights reserved.

Distributed in the U.S. and Canada by Macmillan,
120 Broadway, New York, NY 10271
A CIP catalog record for this book is available from the Library of Congress

Author: Carole Stott
Editors: Catherine Ard and Elizabeth Yeates
Design and styling: Liz Adcock
Cover design: Liz Adcock
Illustrations: Ste Johnson

ISBN: 978-0-7534-7549-2 (HB)
ISBN: 978-0-7534-7550-8 (PB)

Kingfisher books are available for special promotions and premiums.
For details contact: Special Markets Department, Macmillan, 120 Broadway, New York, NY 10271

For more information, please visit
www.kingfisherbooks.com

Printed in China
9 8 7 6 5 4 3 2 1

1TR/1019/WKT/UG/140WFO

WOW!
Look what's in
Space

KINGFISHER
LONDON & NEW YORK

Home, sweet home

Our home is a huge round ball of rock
and metal whizzing through space.

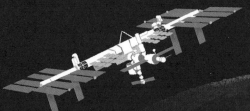

More than seven and a half
billion people live on Earth—
enough to fill ninety thousand
football stadiums. We share our
planet with trillions of other
living things. They live on its
land and in its oceans, and in
the hottest and coldest places.

**Hello down
there!**

If one night you could zoom into
space and look down on Earth,
you would see the bright lights
of cities and towns.

Guess what?

An invisible force called
gravity keeps us on the
ground. Without it, we
would float off
into space.

Hold on . . . we're moving!

Right now, Earth is spinning around faster than a speeding jet plane. We don't feel it moving because Earth is so big. It does a complete turn once every day. It's daytime on the side of Earth facing the Sun, and nighttime on the side facing away.

What's that near Earth?

Wow!

Earth is surrounded by a blanket of invisible gases called the atmosphere. Plants and humans need the gases to breathe and to live.

We Love Earth!

The biggest living animal is the blue whale. It weighs the same as 40 elephants and is as long as three buses.

Next-door neighbor

Meet the Moon, the closest thing to us in space. This big, round ball of rock is the brightest thing in the night sky

The Moon travels around Earth, and Earth travels around the Sun. Wherever we go, the Moon goes too!

Wow!

The dark patches on the Moon are low, flat land and the light parts are hilly lands with mountains. The biggest Moon mountain is higher than Mount Everest—the tallest mountain on Earth!

Which is my best side?

We can only see one side of the Moon from Earth. We know what the other side looks like from pictures taken by spacecraft.

Billions of years ago, space rocks smashed huge circular hollows, called craters, all over the Moon's surface. Some craters are so wide a city could fit inside them.

Some say patches on the Moon look like a face or a rabbit.

What can you see?

The Moon is always round, but the Sun doesn't always shine on all of its round face. We only see the lit up parts. The Moon's fully lit face is called a full Moon.

Full Moon

Wow!
The Moon doesn't make its own light. It reflects the Sun's light, just like a giant mirror. Before street lights, people used moonlight to find their way at night.

whose are these?

On the Moon

Fancy a trip to the Moon? It's a dusty, rocky desert.
There's no air, no water, and nothing living anywhere.

The Eagle has landed!

So far, twelve astronauts have walked on
the Moon. The first two, Neil Armstrong
and Buzz Aldrin, landed in a craft called
Eagle in 1969. Millions of people back
on Earth watched the landing on TV.

Cool shades, dude!

Spacesuits protect astronauts
and give them air to breathe.
The helmet's see-through
visor is lined with real gold to
reflect the sun's harmful rays.

The Moon's gravity isn't as strong as Earth's. There's just enough to pull things to the ground, and stop them floating off. It's best to use long, bouncy strides or bunny hops to get about.

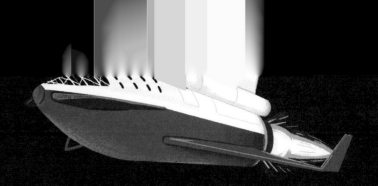

Boing!

It takes about three days to get to the Moon. And three more to get back. Still want to go? It's not such a crazy idea. There are plans for Moon hotels and tourist trips. What do you think a space plane could look like?

Nice shot!

Space sports

It wasn't all work for the astronauts. One astronaut, called Alan Shepard, played a little golf, hitting two balls.

Wow!

All the footprints made on the Moon will be there for millions of years. There is no weather to wash or blow them away!

Space family

Earth is part of a big space family called the Solar System. The red-hot ball in the center is our Sun.

Earth and seven more planets and lots of moons, travel around the Sun in big circles called orbits. It takes 365 days (or one year) for Earth to orbit the Sun.

The four planets closest to the Sun are Mercury, Venus, Earth, and Mars. They are metal in the middle with a thick, rocky coating.

Mars is a rusty red planet. It is half Earth's size and just close enough to visit. But wrap up warm, Mars is further from the Sun than Earth and much colder.

Jupiter is the big brother of the Solar System and 1,300 planets the size of Earth could fit inside it.

YOU ARE HERE!

Sun

Mercury

Venus

Earth

Mars

Jupiter

I'm the biggest planet in the Solar System!

Did you know?

People have known about Mercury, Venus, Mars, Jupiter, and Saturn for thousands of years because they can be seen in the night sky. They named the planets after the gods and goddesses that they worshipped.

Farthest from the Sun are Jupiter, Saturn, Uranus, and Neptune. They are not solid, but enormous balls of gas. If a spacecraft tried to land on one of these "gas giants," it would disappear without a trace!

Wow!

All four gas giants have rings around them. Biggest and most visible are Saturn's. They're made of billions of chunks of icy rock. Some pieces are as small as a grain of rice and others are as big as a bus.

check out my rings!

Saturn

Uranus

Neptune

Rocky rubble

Trillions of objects speed through space. These were left over when the planets and moons were made.

Here come the comets—huge chunks of snow and ice mixed with dust and grit. There are trillions of these dirty snowballs, each one the size of a city. If they travel near the Sun they heat up and grow tails of gas and dust millions of miles long.

Bye for now. See you next time!

Wow!

Pluto lives far beyond the planets where it is freezing cold. It is a dwarf planet and slightly smaller than the Moon. Pluto takes 248 years to travel once around the Sun.

I'm a dwarf planet!

Say hello to the asteroids. Millions of these rocky lumps travel around the Sun between Mars and Jupiter in a ring called the Asteroid Belt. It's a bit like a high-speed racetrack for rocks.

Mars

Sun

Jupiter

Earth

Asteroid Belt

Now and then, two asteroids bang together and pebble-sized bits break off. These are called meteoroids.

Ouch! That hurt!

Some meteoroids travel near to Earth. When they go through its air, they make bright streaks of light in the night sky. These are meteors or "shooting stars."

If a meteoroid makes it all the way down to Earth, it is called a meteorite.

Nearly there!

Wow!

About 3,000 meteorites as heavy as a bag of sugar land on Earth each year. They hit the ground or plunge into the ocean at about 12 miles (20 kilometers) per second.

Supersized

Space is a big place. Our planet is just a tiny pinprick inside an enormous group of stars, known as a galaxy.

Earth

Earth, the Sun, and our family of planets all live inside a huge galaxy called the Milky Way. It's a swirling spiral of billions of stars.

Look how tiny we are!

On dark nights you can spot a milky path of stars stretching across the sky. That is our view of the Milky Way from where we sit inside it.

Wow!

There are billions of galaxies in space. The smallest has 10 billion stars, the biggest 1,000 billion. Ours has 400 billion, but don't try counting them—it would take 12,000 years!

Is that tiny light a star or a galaxy?

Galaxies come in different shapes. Spirals are disk-shaped with long curved arms. Ellipticals are ball- and egg-shaped. Irregulars are uneven, odd-shaped collections of stars.

Spiral

Elliptical
(say i-lip-ti-kal)

Irregular

Did you know?

A galaxy's stars look packed together, but this is because they are so far away. The stars are actually trillions of miles apart.

Galaxies are usually known by letters and numbers. Meet M104, also nicknamed the Sombrero because it looks like a Mexican hat.

Galaxies can get close, and even collide to make new, unusual shapes. Some look like animals. Can you spot the Tadpole, the Porpoise, and the Bird?

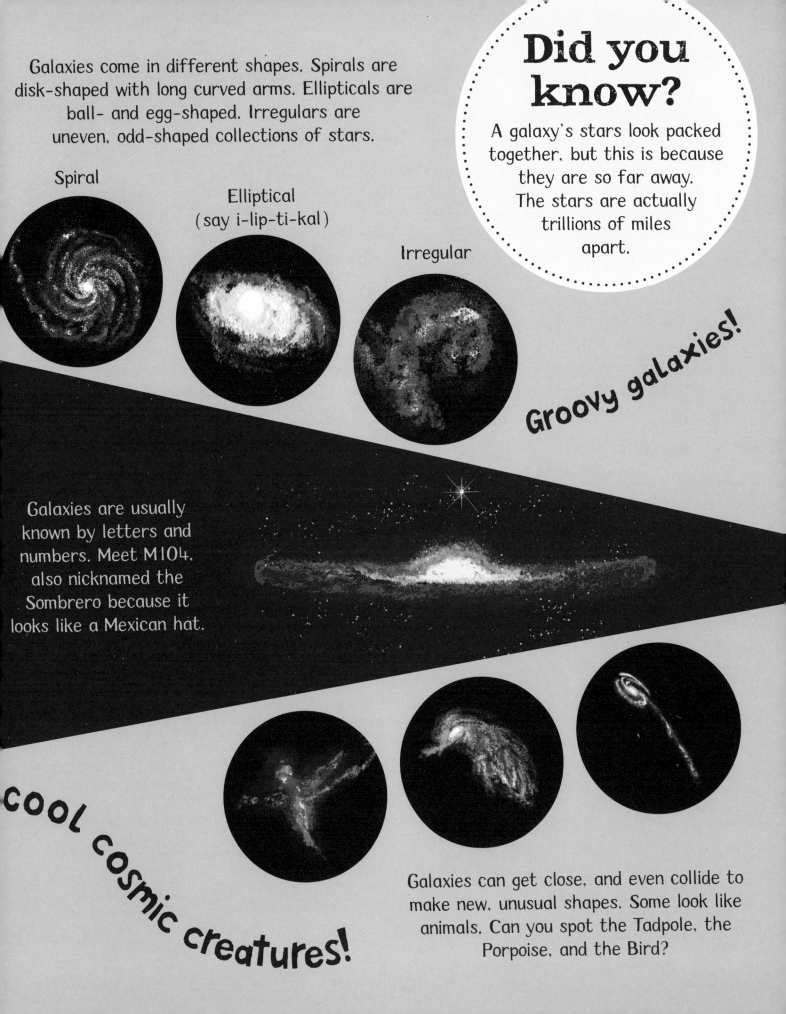

Awesome stars

Stars are huge balls of hot, glowing gas that twinkle in the night sky. The Sun is a star too!

WHEW! Feel the heat!

All stars are super hot. Much hotter than an oven cooking pizza at 400°F (200°C). The Sun is an incredible 10,000°F (5,500°C). It's 93 million miles (150 million kilometers) away but we still feel its heat.

Did you know?

Stars don't twinkle but shine steadily. As the star's light travels through the air around Earth the light wobbles and the star seems to twinkle.

Our Sun could fit more than a million planets the size of Earth inside it. But it is tiny compared with other stars in our galaxy. Next to the star Betelgeuse (say bet-el-jus) our Sun looks tiny!

Sun

Betelgeus

For thousands of years, people have seen pictures in the sky by joining the stars with imaginary lines. These dot-to-dot drawings are called constellations. Many are of animals.

I'm Scorpius the Scorpion.

I'm Leo the Lion.

woof woof!

Wow!
There are more stars in space than grains of sand on all of Earth's beaches.

The brightest stars in the night sky have names. Brightest of all is Sirius. It is in the constellation called the Great Dog.

On a dark cloudless night, you can see about 300 stars in the city sky and about 3,000 in a dark countryside sky. The darker the sky, the more stars you'll see.

Eye on the sky

If you want to get a better look at space, you need a telescope. The bigger it is, the more you will see!

Peering through a telescope makes distant things look bigger. It has a mirror inside it that works like a giant eye, collecting light from stars and galaxies.

zooooom in!

People who study space are called astronomers. They use huge telescopes. The biggest and best telescopes are on top of mountains away from city lights where the air is clear.

Each big telescope sits inside a building. The roof opens when it's time to look into space.

The bigger the better!

Wow!

The Extremely Large Telescope will be the world's biggest when it is finished. Its mirror will be made of 798 giant mirror pieces and the top of its domed roof will be as high as a 24-story building.

...telescopes are in space too, traveling around Earth. The sky is always clear for them and they don't have to wait for darkness to fall, so they can work night and day.

No clouds in space again today!

IS anybody out there?

We also listen to space. Radio telescopes are dish-shaped —like huge ears. They collect radio signals given off by stars and galaxies, which help astronomers understand more about space.

Some radio telescopes send and receive messages from spacecraft. They also listen for aliens!

Space robots

Robot spacecraft discover places in space that are too far away and too dangerous for astronauts to visit.

More than 100 robots have explored space. They fly past planets and moons, travel around them, or land on them.

I was the first robot in space!

Sputnik 1 was the first robot to go into space. In 1957, it traveled around Earth for 22 days before its batteries ran out. It was no bigger than a beach ball.

I'm a long way from home.

Robots Voyager 1 and 2 have been traveling through space for over 40 years! They have taken thousands of pictures of Jupiter, Saturn, Uranus, and Neptune. Now Voyager 1 has left the Solar System and is getting 11 miles (18 km) farther away from Earth every second.

Did you know?

Both Voyager robots carry a message with music and greetings from Earth, just in case they are ever found by aliens.

Juno is on a mission to discover more about Jupiter. This space robot is powered by three big wings that turn sunshine into electricity. It has a camera and eight other instruments for checking out the planet.

I'm sending your photo back to Earth.

Smile!

Wow!

Juno has passengers. Three special Lego figures are on board. They are the Roman god Jupiter, his wife Juno, and the astronomer Galileo.

Robonaut 2 is a human-shaped robot that spent time on the International Space Station. Robonauts help out with jobs that are boring or too dangerous for astronauts to do.

Hi, nice to meet you.

What's this?

21

Roving around

Amazing robotic rovers have driven across the Moon and Mars, discovering more about these far-off places.

Curiosity is the biggest, smartest, and coolest rover to work in space. This car-sized robot is studying Mars' rocks, looking for signs that tiny life forms once lived there. Scientists back on Earth tell Curiosity where to go and what to do.

Curiosity's flexible robotic arm carries an X-ray, a camera, a drill, and a scoop for collecting and examining rock and soil.

Wow!

Six gripping wheels get Curiosity around—but it's a slow mover. It wouldn't win a race with a tortoise.

Curiosity's my name . . . being curious is my game!

Curiosity uses a sort of walkie-talkie to talk to a space object, called a satellite, waiting above Mars. This then sends messages between the rover and Earth.

Curiosity calling Earth...

Earth calling Curiosity...

Did you know?

Two tiny electronic chips on the rover's body contain the names of people who wanted their name to go to Mars—there are 1,246,445 of them!

Curiosity fires a laser beam at far-away rocks. The laser blasts the rock into gas, then the robot runs tests in its onboard space lab to find out what sort of rock it is.

The rover Yutu-2 was the first to rove on the side of the Moon we cannot see from Earth. It arrived inside a lander called Chang'e 4. Also on board were seeds to see if they would sprout on the Moon—some did!

23

Up, up, and away

Rockets blast into space, traveling at 4 miles (8 km) a second! Ready? The countdown has began.

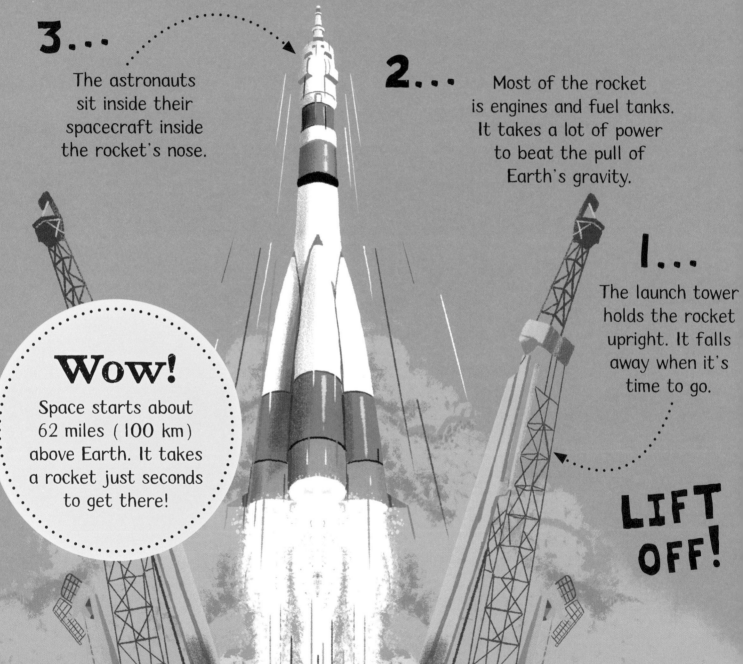

3...

The astronauts sit inside their spacecraft inside the rocket's nose.

2...

Most of the rocket is engines and fuel tanks. It takes a lot of power to beat the pull of Earth's gravity.

1...

The launch tower holds the rocket upright. It falls away when it's time to go.

Wow!

Space starts about 62 miles (100 km) above Earth. It takes a rocket just seconds to get there!

LIFT OFF!

The engines roar as hot gas from the burning fuel whooshes out the bottom.

Astro-animals

Chimps, monkeys, dogs, spiders, jellyfish, and lots of other creatures have all been sent into space.

WOOF!

More than 550 people have been in space. Meet the first man and woman who made the trip.

Yuri Gagarin was the first man to go into space in 1961

Valentina Tereshkova was the first woman in space, in 1963

Time for space walkies!

About two rockets are launched into space every week. Most don't carry people, but satellites. Satellites are machines that travel around the Earth and gather information.

Satellites pass on phone calls and TV signals. With their view of the world, they can watch the weather and help people find their way around on Earth.

Ring! Ring!

Car "sat-nav"

Phone calls

TV signals

We would be lost without satellites!

Living in space

Whose home is 250 miles (400 km) above the ground and travels non-stop around the Earth? An astronaut's!

Astronauts live on the International Space Station, or ISS. It's as big as a soccer field outside, but only the size of a five-bedroom house inside.

Astronauts who stay on the ISS for a few months are slightly taller by the end of a trip. In space, gravity doesn't pull on their body and so they are "stretched" a centimeter or two.

Just popping out to the stores!

When astronauts go outside, it's called a "spacewalk." They wear a spacesuit that gives them air to breathe.

Wow!

A spacesuit takes two and a half years to make and costs about $12 million. It takes 45 minutes to put on!

Astronauts eat, sleep, wash, and work on the space station. There's only one problem—everything floats!

Mission control wakes up the astronauts every morning with music.

"Good day sunshine!"

There's no need for a bed. Astronauts just zip into a sleeping bag. It has to be tied to a wall so they don't drift off when they nod off!

ZZZZ

There are no refrigerators in space so meals are sealed in plastic before a trip. Good table manners are important because crumbs can float up people's noses!

Astronauts wear comfy clothes such as shorts and T-shirts. Clothes are changed about once a week. There's not much room for spare ones, and no washing machine.

27

Hello out there

Could there be more planets like ours, with living things? None have been found yet, but the search goes on . . .

Not long ago we only knew about the planets that travel around our star, the Sun. Now we know that lots of distant stars have planets—they are called exoplanets.

I'm an exoplanet hunter...

Wow!

It would take a spacecraft traveling at over 50,000 miles (80,000 km) per hour thousands of years to reach the nearest exoplanets!

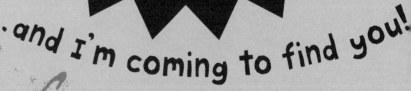

...and I'm coming to find you!

Exoplanets

Star

A space telescope called Kepler was sent into space to hunt for exoplanets. It discovered thousands—and some are a lot like Earth.

An exoplanet needs to be in just the right place for there to be water and living things. Too close to its star and it's too hot, too far away and it's too cold.

what do you think I look like?

Did you know?

Over 4,000 exoplanets have been discovered—too many to give each one a cool name. They are given a letter and named after the star they travel around—like children being named after a parent.

Kepler 186f is a small, rocky, Earth-like exoplanet. It is too far away to see clearly, but it might look a bit like this.

HOT stuff!

55 Cancri e is a super-hot exoplanet twice as big as Earth. It could be covered in bubbling lava like this.

Imagine if exoplanets like Earth had living things on them. Would they be tiny bugs, exotic plants, or intelligent creatures like humans?

Into the future

By the time you are grown up, you might be able to hop on a plane and take a day-trip to space!

A new sort of vehicle—a space plane—is getting ready to take passengers into space. Unlike rockets, which can only make one trip, space planes can land back on Earth ready to be used again.

Fasten your seatbelt!

Imagine packing a suitcase for a holiday in space! Plans are being made to put space hotels about 186 miles (300 kilometers) above Earth. There won't be a swimming pool, but guests can enjoy the finest space food and an amazing view of Earth!

Wow!

American millionaire Dennis Tito was the first space tourist. He paid $20 million for an eight-day stay on the International Space Station.

This hotel is out of this world!

So far, only robots have explored Mars. In the future, people may be able to visit and maybe even live there.

Welcome to Mars!

People could not breathe the air on Mars so they would have to wear spacesuits outside and live in special sealed buildings. Could you make your home on this cold, dusty planet?

It's so space-ious!

Before long, inflatable space stations could be floating in space. Pods made from tough material would be folded up for the trip, then inflated by astronauts once in space.

Super space

The Universe is absolutely everything. It's all of space and everything in it, including you!

The Universe is about 13.8 billion years old, and it has been growing bigger and bigger during all that time.

Remember your space address

Hello from space!

Planet Earth
The Solar System
Milky Way Galaxy
The Universe

Wow!

The Universe is still growing. At breakfast time, it's an amazing 1,553 miles (2,500 kilometers) bigger than when you went to bed.

It all started with an explosion named the Big Bang. Then it was small, hot and made of tiny particles.

BANG!

The particles joined to make stars and galaxies, and the leftovers made planets.

Today the Universe is cooler, bigger, and full of galaxies.

Big wow!

The Universe is so big that light from galaxies takes millions of years to reach us because they are so far away. So we see a galaxy as it was millions of years ago.